THE CRIME
— of —
FAMILY ABDUCTION

A Child's and Parent's Perspective

U.S. Department of Justice
Office of Justice Programs
810 Seventh Street, NW.
Washington, DC 20531

Eric H. Holder, Jr.
U.S. Attorney General

Laurie O. Robinson
Assistant Attorney General
Office of Justice Programs

Jeff Slowikowski
Acting Administrator
Office of Juvenile Justice and Delinquency Prevention

Office of Justice Programs
Innovation • Partnerships • Safer Neighborhoods
www.ojp.usdoj.gov

Office of Juvenile Justice and
Delinquency Prevention
www.ojp.usdoj.gov/ojjdp

This document was prepared by Fox Valley Technical College under cooperative agreement number 2009–MC–CX–K058 from the Office of Juvenile Justice and Delinquency Prevention (OJJDP), Office of Justice Programs, U.S. Department of Justice.

Points of view or opinions expressed in this document are those of the authors and do not necessarily represent the official positions or policies of OJJDP or the U.S. Department of Justice.

The Office of Juvenile Justice and Delinquency Prevention is a component of the Office of Justice Programs, which also includes the Bureau of Justice Assistance; the Bureau of Justice Statistics; the Community Capacity Development Office; the National Institute of Justice; the Office for Victims of Crime; and the Office of Sex Offender Sentencing, Monitoring, Apprehending, Registering, and Tracking (SMART).

First Edition, May 2010

Office of the Attorney General
Washington, D.C. 20530

Message From Attorney General Eric H. Holder, Jr.

Family abduction is the most prevalent form of child abduction in the United States. Regardless of the abductor's motive, it is an illegal act that has lasting consequences for the abducted child, the custodial parent, and the abducting family member. It is a crime in all 50 states and in the District of Columbia.

Written with the help of six persons who have experienced family abduction, this publication features valuable insights from a firsthand perspective. It is designed to provide the searching family, law enforcement, and mental health professionals with strategies to build a comprehensive, child-centered approach to recovery and healing. Above all, this publication was prepared to support victims subjected to the crime of family abduction.

The Department of Justice is committed to protecting children and families from harm. It is my hope that *The Crime of Family Abduction: A Child's and Parent's Perspective* will provide those impacted by this crime with the practical resources and support they need.

Eric H. Holder, Jr.
Attorney General

U.S. Department of Justice

Office of Justice Programs

Office of the Assistant Attorney General

Washington, D.C. 20531

Message From Assistant Attorney General Laurie O. Robinson

Each year, more than 200,000 children become victims of family abduction. Taken from family, home, and friends by a parent or other family member, they are thrust into a life of uncertainty and isolation.

As we work to protect children from harm, we must remain vigilant and informed about the dangers that face children within our communities. A critical part of this responsibility begins with the recognition that family abduction is a serious crime.

This publication was written to provide victims and their families with knowledge and support in their time of crisis. For families undergoing this ordeal, there is comfort in knowing they are not alone and there are resources dedicated to assisting them in the recovery of their abducted children. The hard-earned knowledge provided in this publication came at great cost. May it bear rich dividends in helping others.

Laurie O. Robinson
Assistant Attorney General

Foreword

The abduction of a child by another family member is one of the most devastating crises that a parent could ever encounter. The impact on the abducted child is also traumatic, as he or she grapples with a host of feelings, above all, a sense of betrayal and loss of trust. Nor are these the only persons harmed by family abduction. Brothers and sisters, grandparents, and other extended family, as well as friends are also impacted.

It is for these victims that *The Crime of Family Abduction: A Child's and Parent's Perspective* was written with the help of individuals with intimate knowledge of this crime.

Protecting the well-being of children and their families lies at the very heart of the mission of the Office of Juvenile Justice and Delinquency Prevention. We offer this resource in the hope that it will help victims and their families in coping with the aftermath of family abduction—a crime in every sense of the word. For when we minimize the criminal nature of any abduction, we maximize the trauma experienced by its victims.

Jeff Slowikowski
Acting Administrator
Office of Juvenile Justice and Delinquency Prevention

Acknowledgments

The Office of Juvenile Justice and Delinquency Prevention (OJJDP) is grateful to everyone who devoted their time, energy, and passion to developing this publication, especially those who have experienced firsthand what it feels like to be abducted by a parent or to be the searching parent:

- Liss, Rebekah, Sam F., and Sam M., who are former child abductees.

- Daniel and CJ, who are former searching parents.

- Take Root, a peer-support network for adults who were abducted by family members as children, and its members.

- Team HOPE (Help Offering Parents Empowerment), a family-support network for searching families of abducted children affiliated with the National Center for Missing & Exploited Children, and its members.

- Abby Potash, former searching parent, and Sheri Duncan, former abducted child.

OJJDP also thanks the many professionals who gave their time and effort to find children who were abducted by family members, who have worked to prevent family abductions, and who have put together this publication for searching families and former child abductees. These include consultants Lori St. Onge, Director of Aboriginal Justice, Mi'kmaq Confederacy of Prince Edward Island (PEI) and Case Manager for Child Find PEI; Julie Kenniston, Director of Training and Education, Butler County Children's Services Board, Hamilton, OH; and retired police captain Thomas Smith, Special Crimes Bureau Commander, Collier County Sheriff's Office, Naples, FL. Special thanks go to Ron Laney, Associate Administrator, Child Protection Division, OJJDP, and Helen Connelly and Harriet Heiberg of Fox Valley Technical College for their contributions to the preparation of this book.

The final editing of this publication was performed by Ephy Amoah-Ntim, Tom Cullen, and Brian Higgins of Lockheed Martin's Office of Justice Programs Communications and Publications Support staff. The book was designed and produced by Katherine Lenard of FasterKitty, LLC.

The Crime of Family Abduction: A Child's and Parent's Perspective is dedicated to survivors of family abduction and to those who are still working to recover their missing children.

About This Book

The U.S. Department of Justice reports that as many as 200,000 children are victims of family abduction each year. Although the majority of abducted children are taken not by a stranger, but by a parent or family member, the issue of family abduction remains laden with misconception and myth. Serious missing-child cases that have devastating effects on the child are too often seen as divorce and custody matters, something private that the public and law enforcement should not concern themselves with. The truth is that family abduction can be as physically dangerous and even deadly for the child victims as any other form of child abduction. Most often, however, the worst damage is imperceptible to the eye, occurring deep within the child, leaving traces that may last a lifetime.

This publication offers insights into what it means to be abducted by a family member. Written from the perspective of the child and searching parent, it is designed to help you, the reader, understand the unique characteristics of family abduction and the nightmare that they have experienced. Although the individual circumstances surrounding the authors' cases show the multifaceted diversity of family abduction, the one thing they have in common is that they were all *missing child* cases. The child victims in these cases were concealed by their abductor, hidden not just from their searching family, friends, schools, and community but also from the justice and child protection systems.

The six primary contributors to this document—four adults who were victims of family abduction as children and two searching parents—are active in the missing child community. The former abducted child contributors are members of Take Root, an organization composed of former abducted children that provides peer support and advocates on behalf of child victims. The parent contributors are either members of Team HOPE (Help Offering Parents Empowerment), a support network for parents of missing children, or active with nonprofit organizations that work around the issue of missing children.

Misperceptions about family abduction can potentially cause further trauma to the abducted child. These misperceptions can also lead to an increase in the incidence and duration of family abductions. We hope that sharing these stories will provide a new understanding of the devastating psychological harm and physical dangers that children who are abducted and concealed by family members often face. Our objective is to increase understanding of the crime of family abduction and empower the reader to thoughtfully assist in the immediate and long-term recovery of a child. Whether you are the searching parent, an abducted or former abducted child, a family member, a professional responder, a neighbor, a teacher, or an advocate, you can begin to comprehend what is happening and why a child-centered response, as outlined throughout this book, is so important.

Contents

Society underestimates the impact and implications of children being abducted by parents.

Introduction: Family Abduction Is a Crime

When I was 10 years old, someone took me from the street in front of my home, drove me across the country, gave me a new name, made me lie about who I was and where I was from, and told me I would never go back to my old life or see the rest of my family again.

The strangest part of my story is that I did not realize while it was happening that I was being abducted. A great many people around me responded to the abduction by thinking that it was perfectly okay— thinking, in fact, that the person who took me and hid me for 2 years had a right to do so.

Because the person was my own mother.

—Liss,
former abducted child

The narrative above is only one example of an all-too-real occurrence for too many children and families in the United States.[1] Unfortunately, many people have the same response as the child in the story—they do not realize that family abduction is a crime. They may be reluctant to intervene because they consider it a private family dispute, not a criminal matter.

However, three characteristics distinguish family abduction from a typical custody battle between parents: concealment, intent to prevent contact, and flight. In many custodial interference cases, a parent may make it difficult for the other parent to have access to the child, but in family abduction, the child is hidden and typically forced to live an artificially manipulated life (though sometimes without even knowing it). Even in its mildest form, family abduction places a child in isolation with a distressed caretaker who may neglect the child in terms of care, feeding, and psychological nurturing. As with other forms of abduction, the child becomes a missing child.

---

[1] The Office of Juvenile Justice and Delinquency Prevention's Second National Incidence Studies of Missing, Abducted, Runaway, and Thrownaway Children (NISMART–2) estimate that 203,900 children were victims of a family abduction in 1999. Of this number, a staggering 117,200 were missing from their caretakers. A child can be abducted (i.e., unlawfully removed from custody by a family member) but not necessarily missing. For example, if a child is abducted by a parent and taken to that parent's home in a different state at an address well known to the searching parent, but the taking parent refuses to return the child, that child is considered abducted but not missing.

Recognizing the real harm that a family abduction can have on a child, all 50 states and the District of Columbia have enacted laws[2] that treat family abduction as a felony under certain circumstances. Federal law also prohibits the taking of a child across state lines and out of the country. Many states also have laws that classify family abduction as a misdemeanor offense. Sentencing options may include an order to return the child, community service, restitution, probation, and incarceration.

[2] See *Family Abduction: Prevention and Response* (www.missingkids.com/en_US/publications/NC75.pdf). In addition to providing detailed search and recovery strategies, this handbook provides indepth information about the laws applicable to family abduction. It contains a glossary of terms to help the searching family better communicate with lawyers and the law enforcement community.

Demystifying Family Abduction

Family abduction

- Is a crime.

- Is not a custody issue.

- Is a child welfare issue.

- **Has probable long-term psychological and social effects** on the abducted child.

- **Has traumatic effects** not only on the abducted child and the searching parent but also on left-behind siblings, grandparents, extended family, and friends.

Common characteristics of family abduction

- **Concealment.** The abducting family member conceals the abduction or whereabouts of the child.

- **Intent to deprive indefinitely.** The abducting family member intends to prevent contact between the child and anyone involved with the searching parent for an indefinite period of time.

- **Flight.** The abducting family member transports the child out of state or out of the country to make recovery more difficult.

Sam F's Story

When I tell people that I was abducted as a child they put on a face of dread and concern. Then, when I tell them that my father was the abductor, I immediately hear a sigh of relief. But during any abduction, even if it is by a parent, a child is not just taken away from his parent(s)—the child is taken away from his entire life.

A parent is supposed to look out for your best interest, care for you, and help you grow. A parent is supposed to teach you, nurture you, and put your safety first. It is not easy to put somebody else before you, but that is a job of a parent. But, when parents abduct their son or daughter, they forfeit their right as that child's mother or father. They stop treating their child as a person, and instead, treat their child as a piece of property. My father forfeited that right when he abducted me not only from my mother, but from my entire life.

My father abducted me when I was 10 years old. My parents had been divorced for some time. My mother had custody of me, and I was able to see my father on weekend visitations each month. From my parents' divorce up until the time I was abducted, I struggled with deciding which parent was most important to me. At my young age, I didn't understand what divorce was and thought that since my parents had separated, it made sense for me to choose who I liked the most. While living with my mother, I did chores, homework, ran errands, and had a bedtime. When I saw my Dad four times a month, I went to hockey games, played sports and video games, and watched all the TV I wanted. I had fun when I was with my father. To me, at age 10, it was an easy choice. I loved my father more than my mother. I never questioned whether my father loved me back just as much. A child is not supposed to question whether his parents love him or not.

When I was with my father, I didn't have much to judge life on other than the presents I received and how much TV I got to watch. My father knew this. He also knew how to turn me against my mother. Subtly, my father would tell me that my mother didn't want us to see each other and, more importantly, that my Dad would be put in jail if he didn't pay child support. The only things I took away from this were that my mother was the bad guy, my Dad was the good guy, and that I needed to protect him from my mother. So, when my Dad came to me when I was 10 and told me he was going to run away because my Mom was having him put in jail, he asked me a very important question, "Do you want to come with me?" He told me that if I did not go with him that I would never get to see him again. So, I answered yes. And even though I thought I understood what was going on, I shortly learned that I didn't.

My father paid for the abduction with money my parents saved for me to use for college. Once the money began to run out and the fun was waning, I realized something was wrong. Instead of going to hockey games, playing sports and video games, and watching all the TV I wanted, I was not in school and had no friends. I still got to play video games and watch TV in the apartment, but I wasn't allowed to leave. At this point I realized that my reality was turned upside down and that my new reality was not one I wanted. This is when I realized that whether I chose to go with my father or if he took me, that what I was removed from was not just my mother, but my entire reality and life. I wasn't allowed to use my real name any more. I had a new life and a new past life that was full of lies that I had never witnessed before. The only thing I was in control of was the lies I could tell. I was not allowed to speak of my past. That included my mother, who I had to tell people was dead. Sam and his reality no longer existed. It was now Ben and his reality.

At one point, my father saw how scared I was and realized what was going on. He talked to me about it, asking me to tell him about how fearful I was of the situation and how much I missed being Sam and wanted to go back. His response was to give me money for a bus ticket and tell me that I could go home if I wanted to. I was 10 years old, in Sacramento, CA, while my home, Sam's home, was in New Jersey. He knew I couldn't leave. That is when I began to accept the fact that this was my new life, my new reality, and that I had no choice when I gave up my other life. When I went with my father, I didn't know I was giving up everything. I only thought I was going with my father. This is what was so devastating to me. I thought I was in a safe place, being with a parent, but I wasn't with my parent anymore. I was with somebody who took my life away from me and forced me to live a new one.

When I tell people that I was abducted by my father, after that sigh of relief, their next response is that they are thankful I was recovered and brought back to my mother. But just as quickly as I was taken from my life, my reality, and my mother, I was thrown right back into my life, my reality, and my mother. The problem was that when I was with my father, I had a new life and reality and did not have a mother.

The recovery process felt like I was abducted for a second time. Even though during my abduction I finally felt like something was wrong and wanted to go back, once I returned, I could not go back to being the same person. The major change for my family and friends was that I was abducted and I was missing. Now that I was home, everything should have gone back to normal. That was far from the truth then and is still today. I may have been missing from my friends and family, but every single part of my life was also missing. I was separated from everything I knew and was forced to create a new life for myself. When I was missing, lying became my life, so naturally once I returned home that is all I did. My trust and love were abused by the one person who I was supposed to trust to take care of me. And throughout this ordeal, I asked myself: If my father didn't care about me, why should anybody else? So, I shut down and didn't trust anybody. My entire reality and support network was obliterated when my father decided to abduct me. So when I was home with my mother, my parent who I was brainwashed to hate, I experienced my loved parent's deceit and felt alone.

After 7 years of struggling to find out who I am, I realize I can't. I can't figure out who I am because I am not finished growing. There is so much more to a person than the music he likes or the clothing he wears. All I know is, for the first time in my life, I can respond with the confident answer of at least a name. I am Sam.

I wasn't even allowed to use my real name any more. I had a new life and a new past life. The only thing that I was in control of was the lies that I could tell if I spoke to anybody. I was not allowed to speak of my past and that included my mother, who I had to tell people was dead. Sam and his reality no longer existed; it was now Ben and his reality.

—Sam F.,
former abducted child

Abduction: Being Missing

Imagine this: You are at home with all the things that are familiar to you. You have your family, your pets, your friends, and your belongings. Someone comes into the room and calls you by name, and you look up and answer. You are asked to run an errand with someone you love. You get in the passenger seat of the car. The one you love takes you on a drive to a place you have never seen before. You feel happy.

Then you are told that you can never go back home. You may no longer use your name. Everything is lost to you. You will not see the rest of your family or your pets or your home ever again. All you have left is in the car with you. Everything else is gone. Everyone else is gone. This one moment changes your entire life.

For some children, this is what happens when they are abducted. Other children are taken by a parent who is regularly cruel and abusive. Still others are taken by a family member (an absent father, for example) they do not really know. Yet others are taken to escape real or perceived abuse. Regardless of the relationship the child has with his abductor, in an instant, the child loses everything: the other parent and family members, friends, pets, school, activities, even a family photo or a favorite toy.

This instantaneous loss of community can lead to lasting depression, the loss of a sense of security or stability, a compromised ability to trust oneself or others, and a fear of abandonment.

How Abducted Children Define Family Abduction*

Being scared.

Being betrayed by one of the most important people in your life.

Being scarred.

Learning to create "home" for yourself.

Having no one to depend on but yourself.

A one-way ticket to the loss of childhood.

Missing people you love because of the actions of someone you love.

Being forced to deny the past and create a fictitious one.

Being afraid to love and trust a parent so much ever again and thereby continuing to deny yourself the full relationship you could have with your nonabducting parent.

Not understanding who you are supposed to be and why it's not okay to be who you were.

Wondering if everyone knows you're a liar.

Feeling a huge sadness just under the surface but being afraid to examine it for fear that you'll drown in the sadness.

Moving on and appearing well-adjusted on the outside but feeling tangled up on the inside.

Having wanted a "mommy" for so long and getting her back when you are too old to call her that.

A childhood filled with fear, anxiety, confusion, deception, and alienation.

Wondering how this could possibly be an act of love.

Knowing the abductor hurt you and that you are still in pain now, but not having the physical bruises and scars that show the rest of the world that you have a right to your pain.

Not okay because you were with a parent.

* Responses from members of Take Root. Take Root is a nonprofit support network for adults who were child victims of family abduction.

What Happens to a Child Who Is Abducted?

The sudden disappearance of all that is familiar and loved is only the beginning of the abduction experience for the child. Months or years of a nomadic life may follow, where the child is constantly on the move, continually changing names, and never putting down roots or making real connections. Or, the child and abductor parent may settle in a new community and establish a whole new life under a new identity. Only one thing is certain: while gone, the child is undergoing rapid and significant change. She is becoming further and further removed from the child pictured on the missing-child poster back home.

Because concealment is easier in family abduction than in stranger abduction (it is natural and expected to see a child with her parent), family abduction cases often become measured in months and years rather than days or weeks. The "abduction identity" may, over time, become the child's primary identity. The bonds the child forms and the experiences she has under that new identity can become stronger and more significant than those in the "left-behind" life. And, as the abduction continues, the information the child has been given to explain the absence of missing family becomes ingrained in her mind.

Children who are abducted by family members are often—

- **Courted or groomed by the abducting parent prior to the abduction.** In an attempt to weaken the bond between the child and the other parent, the abductor may spend weeks or even months grooming or brainwashing the child prior to the abduction. This brainwashing may continue well into the abduction, making reunion with the searching parent more difficult when the child is recovered. The feeling that he "agreed" to go with the abductor may cause issues for the child later in life. The child might feel guilty for leaving the other parent or blame himself for going with his abductor. It is important to remember that the responsibility for the abduction rests with the abductor.

My father would tell me that my mother didn't want us to see each other and that she would have him put in jail if he didn't pay child support. In my mind, my mother was the bad guy and my Dad was the good guy. I needed to protect him. So, when he told me that he was going to run away and I would never see him unless I went with him, I said yes.

—Sam F.,
former abducted child

- **Forced to go into hiding with the abductor.** Many abducted children describe their experience as similar to entering the witness protection program. The abductor, in an attempt to conceal the child and avoid any contact with the searching parent, may go into hiding or leave the country altogether.

- **Made to fear discovery.** The child may be taught to fear the very people—police, teachers, doctors—who could help her. In an attempt to conceal the child, the abductor may not allow the child access to proper educational, medical, and social services and support. When this happens, the safety and welfare of the child become compromised and the child comes to rely wholly on the abductor.

- **Given a new name, birthdate or birthplace, and identity.** One way family abduction is more serious than other forms of custodial interference is that the child experiences a sudden change in identity. Abducted children often have their names changed. Some have their looks altered or are even forced to masquerade as the opposite gender. Many are under strict instructions not to reveal their true identifies or circumstances. This ultimately leads to significant issues of identity confusion when the child is recovered. Others may be too young to know or understand the abduction. For these children, the confusion comes later when they are "reunited" with a searching parent or family they do not know or even remember.

I lived with the constant terror that she—we—would be caught and something horrible would happen to us. She taught me to lie and to become invisible to keep our secret. I was afraid that I would be the cause of her going to jail or us being separated. That was the biggest fear of all. Because she was all I had left.

> —Liss,
> former abducted child

I couldn't comprehend what this stranger [an FBI officer] was telling me. My name was Heather, not Rebekah, and I didn't have a father because he did not love or want anything to do with me. That is what I had been told my entire life.

> —Rebekah,
> former abducted child

- **Not encouraged or allowed to grieve their losses.** The abductor's focus is on creating a new identity, so in many cases, the child is forbidden to speak of the past or grieve for lost family and friends. But the loss that the child feels is total, and when the child is recovered, that loss can make it harder and more painful for the child to learn to love and trust the searching parent again.

- **Told to lie about their past.** The abductor may teach the child to conceal the truth about her identity and circumstances. The child may be forbidden to answer the door and told not to play outside, to close the blinds, to hide when riding in a car, to avoid authority, or to evade personal questions or lie. In such situations, distrust of authority may become the norm.

- **Told lies about the searching parent.** The abducted child is often deceived about the searching parent. The child may be told that the parent was so dangerous or violent that the abductor fled to save their lives, that the searching parent did not love or want him, or even that his parent and/or siblings died in an accident.

We were told that our mother was dead. We were also told that there was no reason to be sad, no need for crying, no time for further discussion about Mom.

> —Sam M.,
> former abducted child

Honesty, honor, integrity. When your life has been lived in the shadows and in the realm of deception, you become really good at covering things up, keeping secrets, and telling lies to protect yourself.

> —Liss,
> former abducted child

I can still see my father's face and hear his voice telling me that I was unloved and unwanted by my mother and her family.

> —Jeremy,
> former abducted child

- **Coerced and emotionally blackmailed.** Other times, an abductor tells the child that if the child tells anyone their secret, the abducting parent will be taken away to jail and the child will never see him or her again. Even though the child has been lied to about why the missing parent is gone, she has no way to discover the truth. The only information the child receives comes from the abductor. The child's reality and viewpoints are shaped by what the abductor tells the child. When the child learns the truth after being found again, she may trust no one for a very long time.

- **Kept out of school.** The abducting parent may keep the child out of school to avoid detection. This can hurt the child's academic performance and make it harder for the child to relate to teachers and classmates when the child returns.

My whole world had been shattered, and now I had to start all over. It took a long time for me to trust that my dad was telling me the truth.

—former abducted child

In all, the abductor's actions can have serious emotional, developmental, and psychological implications for the child. The "Recovery" section of this document contains recommendations on ways to minimize trauma during reunification and to help the child move into his new life.

Liss's Story

When I was 10 years old someone took me from the street in front of my apartment building, put me in a car, drove me across the country, gave me a new name, made me lie about who I was and where I was from, and told me I would never go back to my old life or see the rest of my family again. But that is not the strangest part of my story.

The strangest part of my story is that I did not realize, while it was happening, that I was being abducted. And after I was found 2 years later, I would spend the next two decades not certain whether anything out of the ordinary had actually happened. This is because a great many people around me responded to the abduction by thinking that it was perfectly okay— thinking that the person who took me and hid me had a right to do so. Because that person was my own mother.

This one fact caused the people around me—and society as a whole—to use a different set of colors to paint the abduction as something else. It's different for kids who are abducted by nonfamily members; everybody recognizes their abduction for what it is. There are no ifs, ands, or buts about whether something traumatic—not to mention illegal—has occurred.

At the time of my abduction, as I have since learned, friends and family separated into two camps. There were those who thought "poor Herb, how terrible for him for Venetia to take his child away from him like that!" There were others who thought "Poor Venetia, that unreasonable Herb made her life so miserable, it was good for her to get away from him." Nowhere in the mix did anyone say "Good heavens, their child was just abducted!" Terms like "abduction" and "missing child" simply were not used—the situation was minimized, normalized, twisted—even by my own family—into a battle between my parents.

For me, it was more like entering the witness protection program. One day I was a child growing up in New York City where I had been born, part of a loving extended family. The next day, I was a different child who had been born in Virginia Beach with no other family, pulling up at a women's shelter in San Diego, CA. I literally became someone else overnight. Divorce is about watching your parents fight and your family take sides. Family abduction is about your family being eradicated from the face of the earth.

There were many things about being abducted that were hard, including becoming the closest thing to an adult on the scene as my mother descended into emotional collapse after placing us in fugitive isolation. My childhood was over. There was fear all the time—knowing we were always inches away from starving as my mother struggled to earn an income when, because of the fake identity, she had no Social Security number, references, work history, and at first not even an address or phone number. I lived with the constant terror that she—we— would be caught and something horrible would happen to her; that she would go to jail or, as she made me believe, my father would do something awful. And that she and I would be separated. That was the biggest fear of all. Because she was all I had left. My child's brain didn't contemplate that this was so because of her own actions; all I knew was that when everyone else disappeared, she was the only one left standing. She became my everything. Which, of course, was just what she had wanted.

Perhaps the hardest part of all was the grief. Think about what it is like to lose someone you love. Losing one, single, loved one is enough to send an adult into a tailspin. Overnight, I had lost not just ALL my loved ones, but every single person I had ever known in my entire life. Can you even begin to imagine what that would be like? And, I wasn't able to grieve. My mother said she was hiding me because she thought my father would be a bad influence on me and because he was making her life miserable. He was never physically abusive but he harassed her, and she felt like she couldn't take it and no one was going to help, so she had to resolve things herself. So, she abducted me and disappeared. But life as a fugitive was no easier. Soon, she once again felt like she couldn't take it, and no one was going to help, so she had to resolve things herself. She made a plan involving her and me and a car idling with the windows rolled up and a hose attached to the exhaust pipe. Luckily, I'm still here.

I don't know why Mom was able to convince so many friends and family that abducting me was a justified progression in her ongoing battle with my father. Hindsight has clarified for me that my mother was not really acting under a misguided notion of what was best for me as she claimed, but instead operating out of a desire to inflict a mortal wound upon my father. He did indeed go to an early grave, and no one can say how much of a role the devastation of losing his only child and recovering a stranger who hated him played in that.

Sadly, I did not begin to comprehend the full reality of what my mother had done until after my Dad was dead. When he first found us, everything he did confirmed in my mind that he was indeed the enemy—the crazy, dangerous, evil enemy—my mother had made him out to be. If he tried to say that my mother was anything less than a saint who had done anything less than heroic by taking me, it reinforced that he was indeed as crazy delusional as she had said he was. It didn't help that he was an alcoholic who wore his pain and victimhood like a shroud.

I have two genuine regrets in my life, and being so hostile toward my father is one of them. Before Mom abducted me, I was a Daddy's girl. I never once thought of my Dad as dangerous until she told me he was. Recently, members of my mother's family—from who I remained mostly estranged despite having been found because my mother had a vested interest in keeping it that way—have told me that they always liked my Dad. It breaks my heart that they remained silent back then. I can't help but think how much devastation could have been avoided for so many members of my family on both sides if those around my mother at the time had recognized her plan to free herself of my father as an act of child abduction and spoken up against it or reported her to the authorities.

Becoming acutely aware at such an early age that anything can change on a dime is a glass that is both half full and half empty—I simultaneously believe in nothing and everything. I dream big and am frequently successful because I seldom see obstacles as "real" or insurmountable, but then live in constant fear that all I have manifested will disintegrate into thin air. Desperately seeking family, I pull people in, then do my best to push them away, constantly testing whether or not they can be made to disappear. In my world, absolutely nothing is forever.

Or rather, that was the case before my son was born. When we found out I was pregnant, I said to my husband, "I cannot be a Mom. How can I raise a child when I can't even see a future for myself?" But my husband replied, "He will lead the way. He will reach for both our hands, and he will lead us into tomorrow." With the birth of my son came the reality of my union with my husband being truly "forever." Before that, because even my blood ties to my biological kin had not kept us bound, my 11-year marriage had remained a complete abstraction in my mind—a social convention we engaged in for expedience a few weeks after we met because we were citizens of different countries. But rushed and casual as my wedding may have been, I did not marry as either of my parents did. I married someone incapable of separating a child from either of their parents. No one can predict with certainty that my husband and I will never divorce, but I do know that he would never abandon his son. Neither will I, so I now know my husband and son and I all will be in each other's lives as long as the three of us walk this earth. That's a new, huge, solid bedrock to serve as a foundation to who I am. The rest is a work in progress.

Who Abducts?

Children may be taken by parents, family members, or caregivers in a variety of situations. The abductor may be:

- The parent with whom the child lives.

- The parent the child visits.

- A parent whose visitation rights have been curtailed or taken away by a court.

- A parent who flees in response to ongoing family violence or to real or perceived physical, emotional, or sexual abuse.

- An absent parent whom the child has never met.

- A grandparent or another family member or caregiver.

Why Do Parents Abduct?

Parents abduct for a number of reasons:

- The abductor confuses his or her own frustration with the marital relationship with a belief that the other parent is bad for the child.

- The abductor is trying to get back at the other parent by taking away something the other parent "wants" (i.e., the child).

- The abductor is removing the child from *real* physical and/or emotional threat or injury by the other parent.

- The abductor is removing the child from *perceived* physical and/or emotional threat or injury by the other parent.

- The abductor fears the values, influences, or behavior of the other parent.

- The abductor may have never intended to involve the other parent in raising the child.

- The abductor is trying to force a reconciliation with the left behind parent.

Children live in all types of domestic situations before a family abduction. Parents might be separated, divorced, still married, or never married. A child may have a close bond with the parent who takes her or may be distant from or afraid of that parent. The child may not remember or may never have even met the abducting parent. Each case is ultimately different, and the motivations and circumstances that lead to an abduction are complex.

One day, I determined to listen to others because I knew that my judgment was clouded by the emotional turmoil of having my children taken. I learned what support is all about and sometimes where you least expect it. I learned of Team HOPE and gained a sponsor to give me the support of someone who had been in my place. I learned that I had support in the local community from people who gave more than I expected. Early on in the search, someone recommended that I contact the National Center for Missing & Exploited Children. I found their services and experience invaluable.

—Daniel,
former searching parent

*A few years before, my father hit my Mom for
the last time and the divorce proceedings began.
Mom got custody rights, of course, and my
brother and I got to spend fun weekends with
Dad. After one of those visits—to the park or a
museum, perhaps—I asked my mother, "What if
Daddy doesn't bring us back on Sunday?" She
calmed my fears by assuring me that he always
would—the court had ordered it. Not long after
that conversation, my brother and I were
abducted by our father.*

*—Sam M.,
    former abducted child*

My face was pressed against the window and I was struggling to see inside. I had knocked and knocked. I was picking my children up from their summer visit with their Dad, and no one would come to the door. Finally, a window I could see in. The apartment was vacant.

I went from disbelief, to horror, to pain and fear. I remember the glass phone booth——calling my attorney and being told to come home. At that point, I couldn't process it . . . I couldn't think straight . . . I just wanted my babies.

—CJ,
former searching parent

The Search: Looking for the Abducted Child

What Happens to a Parent Whose Child Has Been Abducted?

Imagine this: You go to your child s school to pick her up. You wait in your car. Your child never comes out. You ask the teacher where she is, and you are told that the other parent picked up your child. You begin making phone calls and driving to the other parent s house. **You get there and find it empty.**

The tears became gut-wrenching, snot-flowing sobs that arose from the ground of my being.

—Daniel,
former searching parent

Like the child, the searching parent also deals with tremendous grief and loss. Often, other family members and friends do not know what to do or how to respond. They do not get involved because they view the abduction as a custody battle that should be dealt with privately. But the crime of family abduction requires a different response. The searching parent is often alone trying to deal with the emotional turmoil while also trying to take steps that bring his or her child home safely.

How Searching Parents Experience Family Abduction

It is one thing not to be with one s children. It is an entirely different state of being to not know where they are and how they are, whether they are safe and secure.

I couldn t eat because of the emotional pain and feeling guilty not knowing if my son was eating.

There were days when it was like a raging black hole. I wish I had known to reach out for counseling.

I came to realize that my anger was really a façade for the grief.

I couldn t go to the grocery store. There were too many families there. Too many children who reminded me of my loss.

I was exhausted and burnt out but I was resolved to bring my babies home. I was in a war...there was no time or room to fall apart or give in to my emotions. That came later.

Simple things could bring me to tears. I had to leave professional meetings and conferences at times to get a handle on my emotions. I had to close off my children s bedroom.

Daniel's Story

Years later, I know now that I should have known better—but I didn't. I should have seen it coming. I did but I didn't take heed. She said she was going to do it. I had her threat recorded. But I didn't think that she would follow through. I should have taken more precautions—but I didn't. Then she took our two girls and disappeared in the middle of our divorce. Our children called her "Mommy."

Before the separation, she told me that she would take our girls and move out of state, and I would never see them again. Her threat to disappear came out at the first hearing. I thought that she was going to settle down with the reality of me being the primary caretaker and enjoy the advantages of her single life with her boyfriend. I did not object to her having greater visitation with our girls than the judge allowed. I thought that she loved our children. And I know they loved her.

On a visitation weekend, she did not return our children at 6 p.m. on Sunday as ordered. I started to worry. Sure, I had thoughts that she had followed through with her threats to take our children and run. But I thought it more probable that she would honor the court order. So, I assumed something worse—that she'd had an accident while bringing the girls home. In the back of my mind, I thought she may have chosen to partially ignore the court order and decided to return our girls directly to their school on Monday morning. I called her on her cell phone but there was no answer. After 8 p.m., I started calling the county sheriffs along the route from her home to mine as well as the emergency rooms along the way. At about 3 a.m., I tried to sleep but couldn't because reality kept seeping through my denial of her threats to abduct our children. I got up and began surfing the Web, searching her name, her address, her telephone number to see what popped up. My denial was swept away by what I found. She had posted various things for sale on the Internet in the weeks before. This led to one conclusion; she was preparing to leave town. As the time for school arrived, I had a sick feeling inside as I made the call to confirm that our children were not in school.

In the months that followed, I learned much about myself and my local community. I had been proud and I was humbled. I learned that support surrounded me and was sometimes where I least expected it. I gained a personal understanding of "emotional triggers" because I found that I had little if no control over the emotional roller coaster that I found myself on in my situation as a searching parent. I had to have faith that I would see my children again, so I strove to grasp firmly to hope in their return to my life. A Team HOPE volunteer helped me to hold to that hope, as did my faith. It is one thing not to be with one's children. It is an entirely different state of being to not know where they are, how they are, and whether they are safe and secure.

I was a lucky one. Eventually she returned our children. I don't know why she did, but I suspect that she tired of the "game" of abduction. I decided that it was unproductive and a waste of time to try to figure it out. I decided that it was better to spend time being with my children and attentive to their needs.

It has now been several years since "Mommy" dropped out of our children's lives. I don't understand how a mother could surrender her parental rights. But I decided that for me to attempt to understand the mind of "Mommy" in surrendering her parental rights would require that I understand a mental attitude that I didn't want to know. All I know now is that I am happy to be there to meet the needs of our children.

Checklist for the Searching Parent

When a child is abducted, there are a number of things the searching parent can do to facilitate the safe return of his or her child. The first hours after an abduction can be terribly difficult. Fear, anxiety, anger, and an overwhelming sense of helplessness are real emotions that parents may face. Even through the emotional turmoil and worry, it is important to act quickly. Here are some things to do:

❑ **Confirm that your child is missing.** Search your house and surrounding areas thoroughly. Check with family, friends, and neighbors; check your child's favorite places to go and/or play and ask questions of anyone there; call local hospitals.

❑ **Contact law enforcement.** Ask them to file a missing child report. Law enforcement is required to immediately enter a missing child into the National Crime Information Center (NCIC) Missing Person File. Write down the NCIC number as well as the name, badge number, and contact information of the officer entering the information.

Provide law enforcement with as much information about your missing child as possible, including—

- Date of birth, weight, height, Social Security number, contact information for your child's pediatrician and dentist, name of school.

- A detailed description of what your child was wearing and any personal items in your child's possession at the time of the disappearance. If you can, specify color, brand, and size.

- A list of your child's unique identifying features (e.g., birthmarks, scars, missing teeth, eyeglasses, or braces), speech patterns, and personality traits.

- Recent pictures (preferably taken within the past 3 months). If you do not have recent pictures, ask your child's school or ask friends and family. Don't submit your only copy of a picture because you may not get it back. Make multiple copies of any picture you submit to law enforcement, missing child agencies, and/or the media.

- Your child's completed ID kit, fingerprints, and/or a DNA blood sample if you have these items. Toys and pencils with bite marks, brushes, combs, and hats are also valuable sources of DNA. Turn these over to law enforcement.

Provide law enforcement with as much information about the abducting parent as possible (e.g., contact information, Social Security, credit card, driver's license and license plate numbers, biographical information) along with any pictures you may have of the abductor.

CUT AND CARRY WITH YOU

If you believe your child is in imminent danger of serious bodily injury or death, ask law enforcement to issue an AMBER Alert (www.amberalert.gov). The agency will initiate an alert if the circumstances of the abduction meet the activation criteria.

❏ **Request help and support from trusted friends or family members.** They can help you find your child and ensure you do not overlook or duplicate any steps in the recovery effort.

❏ **Contact your child's school.** Inform them of the situation and flag your child's school records. Under the Family Education Rights and Privacy Act,[1] you have the right to know if your child's records are transferred to another school or if copies are sent to the other parent. Federal law requires school officials to give you the address where the records are to be sent.

❏ **Obtain legal counsel.** If you do not already have a lawyer, ask people you trust for a referral to a family law attorney. You can also refer to the resources in the National Center for Missing & Exploited Children (NCMEC) publication *Family Abduction: Prevention and Response*.[2] You can also obtain a list of family law attorneys from the district court and your state bar association.

❏ **Determine what kind of custody you have** (i.e., joint legal custody, joint physical custody, or full custody). Obtain certified copies of your custody order if you do not already have one from the court that issued the order, and have the court clerk certify that they are true and correct copies of the original. You will need this documentation when you contact law enforcement. It is important for your attorney to work in parallel with law enforcement investigations.

❏ **Consider filing criminal charges and getting a warrant.** You will need to complete a warrant application and attend a hearing in magistrate court. The judge will decide whether to issue a warrant.

   • If the abductor fled the state to avoid felony prosecution, ask the prosecutor for a federal Unlawful Flight to Avoid Prosecution warrant.

   • If the abductor is charged with a felony, ensure that the felony warrant is entered into the NCIC.

❏ **Obtain a pickup order.** Have your attorney request a pickup order for your child as soon as possible. Make sure the order references the Parental Kidnapping Prevention Act (28 U.S.C. 1738). The order should include a clause that expressly states that law enforcement is authorized to pick up the

---

[1] 20 U.S.C. 1232g, 34 CFR Part 99. More information about the Act is available at www2.ed/gov/policy/gen/guid/fpco/ferpa/index.html.

[2] This publication is described in the Resources section.

child(ren) *anywhere in any state*. In-state pickup orders can be enforced in other states and jurisdictions. Each state has their own processes for domesticating orders so they are enforceable.

❑ **Contact the U.S. Department of State's Office of Children's Issues** if there is a chance that the abductor may attempt to take your child out of the country. Fill out a "Request Entry Into the Children's Passport Issuance Alert Program" form and you will be notified of any pending U.S. passport applications (www.travel.state.gov).

❑ **Call the National Center for Missing & Exploited Children (NCMEC)** at 1–800–THE–LOST and report your child as missing.

- Ask NCMEC to confirm that law enforcement entered information for your child into NCIC.

- Contact your state Missing Children Clearinghouse. The NCMEC Web site (www.missingkids.com) provides a directory of state clearinghouses. These clearinghouses provide support and assistance to families of missing children.

- Find out from these missing-child organizations whether you are eligible for state and/or federal crime victim assistance.

❑ **Contact Team HOPE** (Help Offering Parents Empowerment) at 1–866–305–4673. Team HOPE (www.teamhope.org) matches searching families with experienced and trained volunteers who have had or still have a missing child. They will provide emotional support, practical resources, and general assistance.

❑ **Contact the Association of Missing and Exploited Children's Organizations (AMECO)** at 1–877–263–2620 or www.amecoinc.org. AMECO provides services to families with missing and exploited children in the United States and Canada.

❑ **Keep a notebook with you at all times** to write down your thoughts or questions and record important information such as names and telephone numbers.

❑ **Keep your cell phone on and charged at all times.** You should be easily reachable to law enforcement, your child, or anyone with information. Forward your calls to your cell phone when you are away from home.

Your Personal Checklist

❑

❑

❑

❑

❑

❑

❑

❑

✂ CUT AND CARRY WITH YOU

What the Searching Parent May Be Feeling

It can be a lonely time when your child is missing because friends and family don t know what to say.

—Abby,
former searching parent

The taking of a child is a traumatic event that can have physiological and psychological effects on the searching parent. The parent may experience a rollercoaster of emotions. She may be filled with fear, helplessness, and anxiety not knowing where her children are and what is happening to them. The abduction may trigger intense emotions at what may seem like inopportune times, such as when walking through a grocery store and seeing a family with children.

Even as the searching parent worries about his missing child, he must also be the driving force that brings the child home. The search for the abducted child is exhausting, and the stress, worry, and work can cause the searching parent to forget his own needs, even food and rest. The parent may face many road-blocks. Efforts to bring the child home can lead to frustration as the searching parent tries to prove that his child has been taken and concealed illegally and to enlist the help of law enforcement and other professionals. This is when friends and family members are needed.

How To Help the Searching Parent

Friends and family should encourage the searching parent to:

- **Take care of herself.** It is extremely important for the searching parent to remain strong and healthy. In spite of the emotional difficulty the parent faces, it is imperative that she eats, exercises, and gets enough sleep.

- **Seek professional help.** The psychological toll of a family abduction should not be underestimated. Encourage the searching parent to seek counseling, if needed. The National Center for Missing & Exploited Children's Web site (www.missingkids.com) provides a list of mental health professionals who are familiar with issues faced by searching parents.

- **Reach out to family and friends.** Often, searching parents do not reach out for help because they are in shock. If you are able, offer to help print out and duplicate pictures, distribute fliers, fill out applications to missing children agencies, conduct online searches, make meals, handle mail, or provide other assistance.

- **Set boundaries.** Well-intentioned friends and family may try to involve the searching parent in their plans and activities (especially on holidays, the child's birthday, or the anniversary of the abduction). The searching parent should not be pressured into doing anything if she is not ready and should be allowed as much time as is needed before accepting invitations and offers to socialize.

> *Friends want to help—have them come over and divvy up jobs . . . phone trees, posters, research, phone calls, etc.*
>
> *—Abby,*
> *former searching parent*

- **Maintain communication with the abductor's friends and relatives.** The searching parent should not accuse friends and relatives of helping the abductor if she does not know that is the case. It is possible that the abductor's relatives know nothing of the child's whereabouts and are just as worried as the searching parent. They might even help in recovery.

- **Have realistic expectations of law enforcement.** "Tips for Working With Law Enforcement" on page 33 provides information on how searching parents can work with law enforcement most effectively.

- **Take an active role in the search.** Parents need to find something constructive to do during this time to combat feelings of helplessness. Becoming an active part in the search instills hope and a sense of closeness to the child.

- **Hold on to hope.** It is imperative to remain hopeful. Some searching parents find writing in a journal to be a positive way to deal with what they are feeling.

Tips for Dealing With a Searching Parent

If you're a friend or family member, don't say:

- It's not that bad; at least you know your child is with the other parent.

- Don't worry until you have reason to.

- Everything happens for a reason.

- Maybe it's a blessing.

- Why don't you just give up?

- It's probably your fault.

- You have other children, so you couldn't miss one that much.

- I understand/know how you feel.

- Are you going to let your child come home?

- Sometimes you just have to let go.

- How can you go on living?

- You must face that your child might be dead.

- Your child may be better off dead than in a bad situation.

- You should get on with your life.

You need to have a friend or family member who can be there and LISTEN for you. Attend the meetings with law enforcement, the lawyers, the media, everything....You need someone with good ears and who is calm—because all you are thinking about at times are your kids and you may miss things.

—CJ,
former searching parent

If you're a friend or family member, do say:

- You're not alone.

- Never give up.

- There is always hope.

- Take care of yourself, so you can be strong and healthy when your child returns.

- What can I do to help?

- Your children will come home.

If you're in law enforcement or social services, do:

- Return parents' phone calls, keep them informed, and check back with them in a timely fashion.

- Encourage the parent to write down all contacts so that the parent can keep them straight.

- Ask the parent to tell you about the child to help create an environment of trust and caring.

- Help the parent get in touch with advocacy organizations and other resources that can help him or her.

- Listen to the parent. Provide a sympathetic ear. Let the parent vent if he or she needs to.

- Reassure the parent that what he or she feels is normal and acceptable.

- Reassure the parent that you are doing all you can.

- Reassure the parent that he or she is doing all he or she can.

- Give the left-behind parent something he or she can do every day to help in the effort to find the child.

- Encourage the parent to keep a journal of his or her feelings.

- Speak to the parent with kindness, hope, and concern.

- Tell the parent that you'll never give up.

- Enter the abduction into the National Crime Information Center.

Tips for Working With Law Enforcement

Most law enforcement agencies in the United States are small; nearly four-fifths employ fewer than 25 officers.[1] As a result, few are trained to handle the complexities of parental abduction cases, which are often legally complex and highly emotional. Not every case can be handled in the same way. Cases can range from being a civil matter to a major felony or even a federal or international crime.

I was often frustrated because I had false expectations and didn't know the protocol with law enforcement. There are certain protocols and steps, and parents need to know what law enforcement can and cannot do.

—CJ,
former searching parent

Law enforcement officers nationwide increasingly are being taught to emphasize safety and locating the child, even in cases where criminal prosecution would not be successful. The Department of Justice has increased the amount of training and education to law enforcement on these types of cases.

Your contact with law enforcement may be your first direct interaction with law enforcement, ever. Being prepared is vitally important. Here are some things to consider:

- Bring applicable court orders, photographs, and information about everyone involved, including the offender, his or her relatives and friends, and anyone else who might help support and protect the offender or know the possible whereabouts of the child or offender.

- Make sure law enforcement immediately enters your child into the National Crime Information Center Missing Persons List.

- Bring another person with you (except when law enforcement is conducting one-on-one interviews) to support you in these emotional times.

- Remain calm and positive. Don't get argumentative or confrontational, even if the officers are reluctant to take information or a report.

- You may not understand everything taking place during the investigation. Tactics, responses, actions, issues, and problems that develop in the course of your case may be too wide-ranging to discuss in depth. If you do not understand fully, ask.

[1] Federal Bureau of Investigation. Police Employee Data. *Crime in the United States, 2007.* www.fbi.gov/ucr/cius2007/police/index.html

- Think creatively. Leave no stone unturned. Be gently persistent and always work in conjunction with your investigating officer, never on your own.

- Update your child's poster regularly. Changing or using different size photographs, changing the size of the poster itself, or even alternating colors and text fonts will help freshen up your child's poster and make it stand out.

> *You will encounter many empty rabbit holes and dead ends in your search for your abducted children. Maintaining perseverance is a required duty.*
>
> *—Daniel,*
> *former searching parent*

- Take time to know the roles of agencies involved in your case: federal, state, county, municipal, and judicial. Each has a separate yet intertwined role.

- When approached by the media, volunteer search groups, lawyers, and others offering to help, discuss this with law enforcement first.

- Keep a diary of your actions, contacts, meetings, discussions regarding your case.

Tips for Working With the Media

Media involvement in the search for your abducted child can be a double-edged sword. On the one hand, the media can effectively spread the word about your abducted child and ask for help locating her. On the other hand, your private pain now becomes public knowledge.

Remember to write thank-you notes to everyone else who helps you: law enforcement, media, politicians, organizations, etc.

—Abby,
former searching parent

If you decide to involve the media in the search for your child:

• Let law enforcement know of your decision and work with them to ensure that you do not inadvertently release any information that could jeopardize the investigation.

• Be aware that everything you do and say will be seen as a reflection on you and your parenting.

• Coordinate with friends and family to contact a media source on the same day you do to request the story. The media is more likely to publish your story if there is a high level of interest about it within the community.

• Do not say anything negative about the abducting parent; your child may see or hear the broadcast.

• Make your child "real" and memorable to people. Share anecdotes, pictures, and home movies, or ask your child's teacher to create a project around the abduction and have your child's friends write letters to the editor.

• Create a missing child Web site and direct people to the site. Include several pictures of your child and the abducting parent on the site. In the event of a possible sighting, people can visit the site to confirm whether they did indeed see your child.

• You may be approached by people who offer guarantees to find your child for a fee. Be wary of such offers, especially if these people are unwilling to work with law enforcement.

*I wanted things to go back to how they were
before, but I knew I had to tread lightly. She
had been through so much while she was gone.
It broke my heart when she didn't just run into
my arms when I first saw her.*

—former searching parent

Recovery: Finding the Abducted Child

The day has come. Your abducted child has been found. It seems like it should be easy; just pick up the child and bring him home. The reality is not that simple. During the abduction, the abducted child and searching parent both experience the passing of time. The difference is that the child was growing and changing while he was absent from the searching parent. The searching parent remembers the child the way he was at the time of the abduction. This can cause confusion and difficulty when the child and parent are reunited.

To many parents, the recovery might seem like a moment of celebration, but to the child, it may feel like another abduction.[1] The child can feel the same as the day she was taken for the first time if she is simply picked up, moved to a new home, and expected to be someone different (i.e., who she was "before abduction"). In some cases, recovery can become the biggest point of trauma for the child.

> *The recovery process was almost as if I had been abducted for a second time. Just as abruptly as I was taken from her, I was returned to my mother, the parent I was brainwashed to hate, and I felt alone.*
>
> *—Sam F.,*
> *former abducted child*

For some abducted children, the recovery can be even more traumatic than the original abduction. This is especially true in cases in which the child does not know he has been missing.

> *A local criminal attorney called me to tell me that our children had been recovered. I was instantly overcome with an indescribable sensation of "joy." I found myself sobbing and singing almost simultaneously as I drove to pick up our children.*
>
> *—Daniel,*
> *former searching parent*

---

[1] Haviv, L. 2007. Re-framing recovery: An overview of the Kid Gloves Approach to handling abducted children. *Grey Papers.* Take Root.

I had a lot of conflicting emotions and thoughts after we were found. I felt guilty for getting to know my new family. I felt guilty for feeling guilty; I should hate my mother and stepfather for what they did to my family.

> —Sheri,
> *former abducted child*

Imagine this: You were told that your mother is dead. You've lived for years without her in your life. One day someone takes you from your father and puts you in an unfamiliar place and this woman walks in. She looks uncannily like what you remember of your mother but she is older . . . and your mother is dead.

My brother and I were waiting with friends at the bus stop when a car pulled up. In the back seat I thought I saw my Aunt June, my mother's identical twin, inviting us in. Of course, it wasn't my aunt, but my 'dead' mother.

> —Sam M.,
> *former abducted child*

Imagine you have been told that your father is a serial killer. For as long as you can remember, you've lived in absolute terror that he would find you and your Mom. Then, one day at school, you are called into the principal's office. The police are there, along with a man you don't recognize. You're told he is your father. He tries to hug you. You start to scream for help but the police tell you everything will be okay. You begin to cry and ask where your Mom is but all they will say is that everything is going to be okay and your Dad is going to take good care of you. You don't stop crying and yelling for your Mom, but the police put you in a car with the man who leans over, locks the door, and drives you away.

The woman [FBI agent] explained that little girl on the milk carton was me and that I had been abducted for the last 8 years by my mother. She said that my father was on his way to get me and that I couldn't go back home or get any of my things for fear that a family member of my Mom's would try to abduct me again. I was so confused, I instantly began to cry. I couldn't comprehend what this stranger was telling me. I had a different name from the girl on the box, and I didn't have a father. That's what I had been told my entire life.

Without further explanation, the two FBI agents took me to a foster home for the night, and bright and early the next morning, I met my father again, for the first time.

—Rebekah,
former abducted child

The return of our children to my custody began another phase in their separation from one of their parents.

—Daniel,
former searching parent

For some children, the experience of being reunited with the searching parent is not as negative. However, the child could be dealing with confusion, fear, anger, helplessness, loss, and many other emotions in addition to joy and excitement. How does a child process all that information, especially when others are standing around celebrating the child's return?

Because a poorly handled recovery can mimic the original abduction, it is imperative that the recovery be carried out with a child-centered focus. Recovery of the child and reintegration into a family should be a process that unfolds slowly and in a manner befitting the child's best interest.

Planning for Recovery

The process of recovery is not as simple as it sounds. There are a number of important steps that should be followed to help and support the child throughout this process.[2]

I Research—Gathering information about the common effects of abduction and about the specific circumstances surrounding an individual case to determine the best recovery plan.

There are many options to consider, and parents, law enforcement officers, and others aiding in the child's recovery should prepare for several possible outcomes. The child might be overjoyed to see the searching parent and ready to go home with him right away. Or, the child may need time to absorb and process new information before being placed with the searching parent. In these cases, safe family members, friends, foster parents, or local child protection agency resources may need to be identified for possible placement options until the child is ready to be placed with the searching parent.

The child will need therapeutic support while she is growing accustomed to the return to her family. A mental health professional should be selected to assist in the recovery process. The searching parent has to be mentally and emotionally prepared to recover a child who may be fearful or hostile.

A plan should be made for the eventual transfer of the child's possessions beyond what the child is able to pack and bring when removed.

A plan for ongoing contact with safe people in the child's life (step- and half-siblings, friends, teachers, etc.) also should be made prior to the removal so that the child understands that his life is not being taken away forever.

All of these things should be considered and planned out before the child is removed from his abduction life.

I was happy to see my Mom again, but I remember wishing it could have happened the next day because then I would've had the cool figurine with me for "show and tell" that I had saved months worth of cereal box tops to get. Plus, I could have said goodbye to my Dad and friends, none of whom I've ever spoken with since.

—Sam M.,
former abducted child

[2] Adapted with permission from Take Root's *Kid Gloves for Handling Abducted Children* (www.takeroot.org/publications.html).

2 **Removal**—Physically taking the child from her current home.

The removal of the child from the abductor should be handled gently, in a private location, without sirens or guns and with plainclothes police, if possible. The child is unexpectedly being asked to change everything . . . again. If the child has been living under a different name, everyone involved should use the name with which the child is most comfortable. The child should be given time to pack belongings and to say goodbye to people in her life. She deserves closure.

Who first approaches and removes the child (and how) should be thoughtfully planned out. The child should have a trained mental health professional as a support person during the removal to explain what is happening in a developmentally and clinically appropriate manner. In addition, everything possible should be done to avoid having the child witness the arrest of the taking parent. In some situations, it may be in the child's best interest to be afforded the opportunity to say goodbye to and receive reassurance from the abductor; however, this must be evaluated on a case-by-case basis.

I was profoundly moved and I am still to this day very thankful for all who made the recovery possible and did so with little trauma. The children didn't witness their mother being arrested.

—Daniel,
former searching parent

3 **Reassessment**—Determining the child's immediate emotional and psychological needs and readiness for reunion.

In most cases, there is a prevailing assumption during the search phase that the child will likely go home with the searching family immediately after being removed from the abductor. This must be reevaluated once a qualified professional has gently probed the child's beliefs and memories of the left-behind family while explaining the situation to the child during the removal phase. In terms of the child's immediate emotional and psychological needs, recovery should be seen as a chance for discovery, and assumptions must be replaced with assessment. The results of this quick, initial reassessment determine the pace and manner of the reunion meeting.

4 **Reunion**—Structuring and facilitating the child's first meeting with the searching parent.

The reunion can be emotional, and the child and the searching parent may experience it differently. The first meeting should take place in a controlled environment and be facilitated by a mental health professional, with ground rules established in advance. These can include a mechanism for the child to signal if he feels overwhelmed and needs to take a break. In some situations, it can be advisable to offer the child simple choices to restore a sense of empowerment—choices such as who should attend, where everyone should sit, or which game the child would like to play as everyone gets reacquainted. Other times, even simple choices may overwhelm the child. The mental health professional who has been working with the child during

41

the removal and reassessment should make the determination.

The child should be given as much information as is available about what will occur and what will happen when the meeting is over, while the searching family should be informed about the child's frame of mind and what is likely to elicit the best response. The number of attendees should be limited so as not to overwhelm the child, and the media should never, under any circumstances, be involved. Everyone should continue to use the name with which the *child* feels most comfortable.

5 Return—Transferring the child's care and custody to the searching parent.

Based on the child's experiences while away, it might be recommended that the child be placed in a transition environment for a time prior to the return. The environment into which the child is returned should be warm, friendly, and welcoming to the child and should soothe the child's fears about leaving the abduction environment. The environment must give the child a sense of safety and should not exacerbate trauma for the child. The research phase should include a plan for transitioning the child to the searching parent if the child is not ready to be immediately reunited with and/or returned to the searching family.

For years, I struggled with trust, identity, relationship, and self-esteem issues that stemmed from my abduction. All my mom wanted to do was help me, but I wouldn't let her in. How could I trust her when I had been so badly betrayed by my other parent?

—Sam F.,
former abducted child

What To Take When You Pick Up Your Child

Prepare a bag to have ready when you go to pick up your child. The bag should contain:

- Several certified copies of the court order.

- Snacks in case you have a long journey and your child gets hungry on the way home.

- Cash in the event that you have short notice and do not have time to stop at a bank.

- A change of clothes for both you and the child.

- Stuffed animal or familiar toy (for a young child).

- Pictures of the child, siblings, and/or pets. (Note: Although some children will appreciate pictures, others may feel manipulated, so if you bring pictures, ask the child first whether she is interested in seeing them before pulling them out.)

Sam M's Story

My brother and I weren't abducted. We got to "go on a 2-week vacation with Dad in Canada!" My older brother was 10 at the time and fondly remembers hockey games with our Dad. At age 6, I was more excited by the snow and ice-fishing. Sometime during that short vacation, Dad told us that our Mom died, so we were "going to get to stay with Dad all the time now. Wouldn't that be fun?" No reason to be sad, no need for crying, no time for further discussion about Mom. We were too busy moving from place to place across the country.

A few years before, my father hit my Mom for the last time, and the divorce proceedings began. Mom got custody rights, and my brother and I got to spend fun weekends with Dad. After one of those weekends, I asked my mother, "what if Daddy doesn't bring us back on Sunday?" She calmed my fears by assuring me that he always would—the court had ordered it. Not long after that, of course, is when our "extended vacation" began in March 1969.

By the summer of '69, Dad, my brother, and I settled into a small apartment in Seattle, WA. My brother and I started going to school again, and Dad's girlfriend from home somehow was in Seattle too and began living with us. She kept asking if we wanted to call her "Mom," but even though we thought our Mom was dead, that was still out of the question. My brother and I established friendships, raced the bus to school some days, and got wet a lot in the Seattle rain. Life seemed fairly normal to 6-year old Sam.

Meanwhile, back in Pittsburgh, PA, our Mom was going crazy trying to find us. She had a job but still worked day and night trying to get us back. She made phone calls, sent thousands of letters, hired private investigators, alerted the police, FBI, media, everyone, anyone. She even wrote to J. Edgar Hoover and Pat Nixon.

When the flier first arrived at our school in Seattle, the principal didn't recognize us. But several months later in December of 1969, the folder containing our photos fell open in his office while the assistant principal was there. He instantly recognized us. They were hesitant about what to do, since they didn't know who was the good guy or bad guy in this scenario. Fortunately, they phoned Sergeant Rocco, who called my mother and said, "We found our boys." Mom leapt into action. She flew to Seattle on the next plane with a private investigator (PI). That night, she could see us through our apartment window, but the PI wisely made her wait until the time was right. The next morning, my brother and I were waiting with friends at the bus stop when a car pulled up. In the back seat, I thought I saw my Aunt June, my mother's identical twin, inviting us in. Of course, it wasn't my aunt, but my "dead" mother. We went straight to the airport where Mom hid us in the ladies' restroom fearing that someone would spot us. I was happy to see her again, but remember wishing it could have happened the next day because then I would've had the cool figurine with me for "show and tell" that I had saved months' worth of cereal boxtops to get. Plus, I could've said goodbye to my Dad and friends, none of whom I've ever spoken with since.

My mother chose not to put us through any more trauma and opted not to press charges.

Instead, she got a restraining order against our father. I never got to talk to him as an adult. I'm not certain why my father took us from our mother. I suppose there was some amount of love involved, but more than likely, it was just another way to hit her after the divorce. I don't know if he regretted taking us or even losing us.

I grew up determined not to use what happened as a crutch, but instead became fiercely independent and active: Senior Patrol Leader of my Boy Scout troop, paperboy at age 11, captain of the high school soccer team, president of my college fraternity, etc. My brother's life has been tougher. The effects on him are more obvious. He bonded more with our Dad and believes himself to be the "spitting image" of his father, bad traits and all. My brother can't always be counted on to tell the truth, and he's had trouble holding a job. He blames himself still for things he did or did not do during our "time with Dad." Perhaps, he should have called someone in the family or told Dad's girlfriend off for suggesting she could be our "mother."

Though the impact on my life wasn't as evident initially, over time, I have come to learn how being abducted by my Dad and reabducted by my Mom has affected my life. For the longest time, I thought the best way to deal with what had happened to me as a child was just to forget about it. Push it into the past and leave it alone. Move on. I denied it had any effect on my life, but in fact, I convinced myself that it had made me stronger. More independent.

I'm not sure what made me agree to go to that first-ever meeting of adults who had been parentally abducted as children at the National Center for Missing & Exploited Children in March of 2002. Perhaps it was a combination of curiosity, a promise to an involved friend, the free trip to D.C., the chance to help others, most notably my own brother, but certainly not to resolve any issues for myself. Or so I thought.

It turns out I had been suppressing thoughts and feelings about my childhood abduction ("kidnapping," we called it then). It turns out that talking about it as much as I have has made me feel better about myself, lighter inside. And, hearing the stories of others who have gone through the experience has made me more aware than ever of the many, many possible effects from parental abduction. Some of the other stories made me actually feel fortunate that my situation wasn't so bad. Learning from professionals about the ramifications has opened my eyes and heart as well.

Take Root has created a safe environment for adults who were parentally abducted to encourage introspection and learning. My biggest "aha" from talking about my hidden secret to so many, though, has really had little to do with me or parental abduction. By sharing my deep, dark story, I've come to learn that nearly everyone, almost to a person, has responded by opening up to me to share the tragedy of their life. Anorexia, alcoholism, lost parents, rape or sexual abuse, the list goes on and on. So many of us have not had anywhere near a perfect life or childhood. It's just that we all think we are the only ones with a sad secret. Opening up to others has brought me closer to people—family and strangers—than I had ever been capable of being. Finding out we are not alone, and being encouraged by the fortitude of others, has been my biggest blessing.

Managing the Aftershocks

Even after I was recovered and in the loving hands of my rightful family, I remained plagued by various paralyzing fears—

- *Fear that I would be taken again and that my security could end again at any moment.*

- *Fear that I was unlikable and unlovable to anyone (save my immediate family), which resulted in me being fairly socially reclusive until college.*

- *An irrational fear that people I love would die unless I was with them at all times.*

Furthermore, as I entered adulthood, I discovered that I struggled to trust the loyalty of others. I questioned the strength of friendships and romantic relationships, often alienating others because of my own poor self-image.

—Jeremy,
former abducted child

The effects of an abduction on a child depend on a variety of factors, including the length of the abduction, the age of the child, the events that occurred during the abduction, the way in which the child dealt with the abduction, and the manner in which the recovery was handled.

Immediate and/or long-term issues that commonly surface in survivors of child family abduction include feelings of loss, anger, shame, loneliness, insecurity, and being unloved; confusion about identity; and a fear of loss and/or commitment. Family abduction survivors may also have trouble telling the truth from the lies the abducting parent told them.

Parents, family members, friends, and teachers must recognize that the child who returns is different than the one who was taken. The child has had many experiences while gone—not all of them bad—and should be allowed to be his true self, even if that true self is different from the searching family's "usual" way.

- The returning child has many things to deal with: parents, family, siblings (maybe even some new ones), friends, and community. Everything will be different.

- The child may have a changed identity as well as a new name.

- The child may go from an only-child family to a new, larger family, making the transition even more difficult.

- The child's educational situation may change —the child may be placed in a different grade level and probably a totally different school setting.

- The abducting parent and searching parent may have different rules, expectations, and ways of parenting, creating confusion and anxiety for the child and the family to whom the child is returning.

- The returning child will probably have a totally new living environment—home, family, school, community, even the area of the country.

- The abduction was not just an event but an ongoing experience that changed the child's whole life.

- The abduction is about the child and what he has experienced—sometimes this is lost in the process.

- There are developmental issues unique to abducted children that should be paid attention to:

  - The child may have been forced to grow up before her time.

- The child may have missed out on milestones such as birthdays, holidays, and school promotions.

- The child has been constantly starting over—new schools, new residences, new classmates and acquaintances.

- There is no continuum—the child may have been forced to assume a new identity, often several times over.

- The child may lag behind emotionally and educationally.

- The child operates in survival mode.

- The child loses his childhood.

- Abnormal things may have become normalized, such as hiding in the car, keeping curtains closed all the time, keeping lights off, not answering the door, and continual moving from location to location.

I'm sorry I will never be the child you would have raised . . . One thing that was always so hard for me was that I knew they felt (because they have even said it at times) that if I had grown up there I would probably be more like them. Yes, I probably would. And in some ways that would be great. In other ways, I'm proud of who I became.

—former abducted child

How To Minimize Potential Pitfalls When a Child Is Returned[1]

I wish I knew then what I know now so that I could have better managed the challenges we all faced when the boys returned to me. They were home and I just needed to protect them. I had no idea we all needed help.

—CJ,
former searching parent

The returning child is not just returning to the searching parent. The child will need to assimilate into a new school, extended family, culture, and community. Parents, family members, friends, and teachers must acknowledge that the returned child is different from the one who was taken. The focus should be on *helping the child* gradually repair his ruptured identity, transition from the abduction identity to the new life, and rebuild relationships. There are many ways to foster the transition between the two identities so recovery does not become another point of rupture for the child.

- **Provide access to qualified mental health counseling.**
The child should have his own therapist, someone who is skilled in working with traumatized children. The therapist should complete an assessment of the child's mental health status and may recommend individual therapy for the child and/or family therapy. Because the child may be experiencing conflicting loyalties, it will be important for him to have his own counselor to help deal with both the abduction and the recovery. At the same time, good family therapy can help the family better understand the child and help the child and family integrate.

When I finally found a safe environment with a therapist I trusted, it was wonderful to have a neutral place to go and not be guarded or embarrassed by my feelings.

—Rebekah,
former abducted child

[1] Haviv, L. et al. 2007. *Handling Abducted Children: Kid Gloves for Left-Behind Parents.* Kalama, WA: Take Root.

- **Allow the child to set the pace.** As the child begins to integrate the "new reality" into her life, she will also be coming to grips with the loss of the old reality. It can take time for the child to accept that a trusted, beloved parent was lying to her. And it may be scary to let go of a parent on whom she has been completely dependent. Giving the child the time, space, and appropriate professional mental health assistance to reconcile the two competing views is crucial. Attempting to push or force the child into the "new reality" simply mirrors the abduction experience. The child should set the pace for sharing both details about the abduction and affection toward the searching family.

If I could say one thing to my Mom, I would just ask her to please hear me. Don't change the subject if I want to talk about what happened. Don't try and make me feel crazier than I already do, and I don't want or need to hear about how bad it was for her when I was gone. I know that sounds harsh, but sometimes it's so hard. I've spent so long taking care of her, taking care of my Dad, pretending like I'm fine and that my life was 'normal.' If I stray from that . . . if I talk about how confusing it was to be moved from state to state, to never have friends, to think that my Mom didn't care about me . . . then that's not acceptable to hear. If I talk about my pain, then I'm somehow negating her pain of being left behind. I want to know that my Mom, the one who loved me and cared for me so many years, still cares that I'm hurting and wants to hear about what happened to me. I want her to hear me.

—former abducted child

- **Do not take rejection personally.** The child might be wary of, act negatively toward, or reject the searching parent. The searching parent should remember that he is asking for the child's trust just as the child is being confronted with the consequences of an enormous breach of trust by his abductor. It will take time for the child to trust again.

- **Set clear expectations. Provide structure and discipline.** During the abduction, the child may have been encouraged to lie or keep secrets. She also may also have become accustomed to a lack of adult supervision. Giving the child clear messages about how things are done in her new home will reduce confusion about the new behavioral expectations.

- **Acknowledge the trauma the child has been through.** The child will face tremendous pressure to present herself as being "okay" when he returns, often in ways that are not evident to the parent or family members. The pressure can come from a desire to protect the family from further worry, a desire to fit into the family or other social settings, or as a response to cues all around him telling him that being "okay" now is what is expected. He may suppress the abduction as a means of protection and survival, just as he learned to suppress the left-behind life during the abduction.[2]

- **Do not say negative things about the abductor in front of the child.** A child's relationship with the abductor does not disappear into thin air. There has been a bond—be it healthy or dysfunctional—that must be considered in postabduction planning. There may be circumstances where it is safe and beneficial for the child to have some ongoing contact with the abducting parent. In other circumstances, it may not be possible or advisable. This can be thought through with the help of a mental health professional. But it is important to recognize that the child will have his own feelings about the abductor, which may be negative or positive. Denigrating the abductor or trying to persuade the child to see him in a negative light can mirror the abductor's actions and may make the reunion more difficult.

> We were expected to be happy that the ordeal was over. And so I learned to try to pretend that everything was okay. So that I didn't hurt anyone's feelings, I learned to hide some of my own.
>
> —Sheri,
> former abducted child

> Your child might voice thoughts about the other parent that may be positive. As difficult as it is for you, give them the space to do that—give your child the freedom to love both parents; don't make them choose sides. This will actually bring you and your child closer and your child will be able to trust you with their innermost thoughts and feelings.
>
> —Abby,
> former searching parent

---

[2] Haviv, L. 2010. A typology of family abductions. *Grey Papers*. Take Root.

Helping Your Child Adjust to a New Home

Children *do* get found and they *do* come home. When this happens, the searching parent is often overjoyed and ecstatic. However, the searching parent needs to recognize that the child has just been pulled from the life she was living and from the parent she depended on, whether the situation was good or bad. Now the work of getting to know one another begins. This requires patience and understanding. **How reunification is handled will influence the child's connection with the searching parent for a long time.** The searching parent should acknowledge that the child still has connections with her former life and judiciously allow her to maintain those connections while creating new routines that add stability to the child's life and help to strengthen the ties to her new home.

- Let the child use the name he prefers.

- Encourage her to continue activities she was involved in during the abduction, such as scouts, soccer, tumbling, and softball.

- Encourage her to keep in touch with friends she made, as long as it is safe.

- Be creative—for example, if the child was taken to a city where he became a fan of the local team, get that team's pennant for his room.

- Keep the child's life structured, organized, and disciplined, but give her choices that empower her—even if it is the smallest of choices, like "Do you want eggs or cereal for breakfast?"

- Make a chronicle of what happened while the child was gone and let him know he is welcome to read it. Write down what steps were taken to find the child. Include pictures of important family events like new births or graduations or bringing the family dog home as a puppy.

- Above all, encourage the child to freely express all her memories from the abduction identity, both good and bad.

I wish I had stuck with therapy much longer than I did. I wish I had faced the fears, anxieties, and paranoia early on rather than repressing them.

—Rebekah,
former abducted child

Rebekah's Story

It was like any other day sitting in my fifth-grade classroom in Eureka, CA. I was dreading the math problems the teacher just assigned when the principal walked into class and abruptly asked me to come with him. I remember walking to his office. He was looking at me weird, like he didn't recognize me, and the silence was deafening. I was so nervous. I started running through all the things I might have done to get me in trouble and be pulled out of class by the principal himself. We arrived at the main office and he asked me to wait in the reception area for a minute. He went inside his office and shut the door. After a few minutes, I heard his footsteps on the other side of the door as he opened it to escort me in.

In his office, I found two "suits," two police officers, and one nicely dressed woman. The woman was sitting on the couch, the police stood by the door, and the suits were by the desk. The woman asked me to sit by her and I did. I was completely freaked out and nervous. I didn't know what to think. Just as I sat down, the woman introduced herself, followed by the two FBI agents and the two police officers. To this day, I cannot remember their names. Before I had a moment to ask any questions, the woman pulled out a flattened milk carton with a picture of a little girl on it. The woman asked me if I knew who the little girl was, and I said no. She explained that little girl was me and that I had been abducted for the last 8 years by my mother—and that my father and the FBI had been looking for me ever since. But my name was Heather! I was so confused. I instantly began to cry. I didn't know how to comprehend what this stranger was telling me. My name was different. I did not have a father because he did not love me or want anything to do with me. This is what I thought my whole entire life. I truly didn't know what to think or feel, so I asked for everyone's identification. In retrospect I know it is funny—a 12-year-old girl asking the FBI and police for their credentials. None of this made sense to me. How do I deal with being told that my whole life is a lie? The woman told me my father was on his way to get me and that I couldn't go back home or get any of my things for fear that a family member of my Mom would try to abduct me again. Without any further explanation, the two FBI agents took me to a foster home for the night and early the next morning, I met my father again, for the first time.

After I was reunited with my father and siblings, my mother was arrested, given a felony, and put on probation for 7 to 10 years. Though it sounds like my Mom got judicial justice, her stay in jail was 2 days, and her probation was never followed up—she left Illinois numerous times even after she was ordered not to. Emotionally, I was angry and resentful toward her. I hated her for lying to me and for what she did. She took me away from my childhood and my siblings. She robbed me of my "normal" childhood and the love of my father and siblings. Along with the anger came confusion. I didn't have any grasp on reality or what was emotionally real around me. I didn't know who or what situations to trust. All I could do was seek answers as to why this happened to me. Little did I know I was never going to get them. I was asking these questions of my mother, the one person whose reality and word I could not trust. Her answer was simply, "I was protecting you and taking you out of harm's way."

My retort was always the same, "that is another lie because if that were true, you would have tried 'saving' your other children as well, unless, of course, you just didn't love them or care if they were in danger." Anger and confusion manifested itself in many ways. The most harmful way was that I did not know how to be Rebekah without emotionally and mentally killing my namesake Heather. I had a new life now, a new reality that had a swarm of people who loved and supported me. How can I be Heather in that? Everything from my former life was lost and gone. I didn't live in the same state, didn't have my friends, didn't have any of my possessions, and didn't have my mother. I now had siblings, a father, a cat, real Converse shoes—and all of these things came literally overnight. Not one thing in my life was the same other than I was physically me.

I look back on my first life and can't remember much, including names and faces of important people to me at the time because not only was I not allowed to take anything from that life but I felt I was forced to bury it to become who I really was, which was Rebekah. Who is Rebekah? To this day, I still don't always know. I have struggled my whole life to identify with the one person who should be innate—me. I never had a reality or foundation to start from to create that. Yes, I had a loving and supporting family, but that was outside of me—that is not who I am. That enriches my life but does not create it. I have never had the confidence long enough of being one person to build who I am and my own identity. The fact I am an adult survivor of a childhood parental abduction has become my identity now. It is the only thing that makes sense to identify with.

This is the reality my mother created for me. A reality based on lies so deeply rooted that as a human being I can't identify with myself internally and externally in the world around me. I do not want to sound so emotionally severed from myself as to suggest I have not made strides at self-awareness and identification because I have. In ways, I feel I know myself emotionally within the constructs of my abducted identity more than most people know themselves in a whole life-time. But my struggle is who would I have been without this rupture? Who am I authentically without the alienation, anxiety, fear, paranoia, and self-doubt? How do I become that person I know I can be without those limitations on my life as my default? I don't want to waste any time regretting my past and that's why I have always tried to make the most of my present and future. Not a day has gone by that I feel I have emotionally or mentally been able to do so because of the trauma I went through. What limits would I have if I didn't have those of my identity crisis? I honestly think not many. I was robbed of a life without perpetual innate anxiety, fear, alienation, anger, and paranoia as a default state of mind. At this point, I don't think I would know how to live without those things, and the fleeting moments it does happen are the most insecure.

Final Thoughts

Family abduction is a crime that has lasting effects on those who experience it. Understanding what it is and its potential outcomes can help professionals and those who work with abducted children and searching parents respond appropriately, thereby reducing further victimization and trauma. In the earlier sections of this document, the realities of family abduction have been described through the eyes of the abducted child and the searching parent. Their words provide insights into what it means to be abducted by a family member and, in doing so, offer professionals and volunteers the knowledge and information they need to support others facing similar situations. The contributors hope that by sharing their stories and thoughts, they can empower law enforcement professionals, social workers, volunteers, and others to make a difference.

Things do get better with time if you make the effort to work through things and face yourself and your fears.

—Rebekah,
former abducted child

This section contains resources for missing and abducted children and their families.

Resources

This section provides information regarding additional publications, programs, and resources that focus on and support missing and abducted children and their families.

Publications

The following selected publications relating to child abduction are available online from the Office of Juvenile Justice and Delinquency Prevention (OJJDP), the National Center for Missing & Exploited Children (NCMEC), and Take Root.

A Child Is Missing: Providing Support for Families of Missing Children
This handbook provides professionals who support families of missing children with information about the needs of and ways to support the missing child's immediate family members, extended family members, friends, and others from the time the child is determined to be missing through the hours, days, weeks, and years of the absence.
(NCMEC, www.missingkids.com/en_US/publications/NC172.pdf, 56 pp.)

Family Abduction: Prevention and Response
This handbook contains step-by-step information for those who have experienced a family abduction—whether domestic or international. It was produced in cooperation with the American Bar Association. The handbook guides families through the civil- and criminal-justice systems, explains the laws that will help them, outlines prevention methods, and provides suggestions for aftercare following the abduction. It also details search and recovery strategies and contains valuable advice for attorneys, prosecutors, and family-court judges handling these difficult cases.
(NCMEC, www.missingkids.com/en_US/publications/NC75.pdf, 244 pp.)

Family Resource Guide on International Parental Kidnapping (Second Edition)
Presents practical and detailed advice about preventing international kidnapping and increasing the chance that children who are kidnapped or wrongfully retained will be returned. This OJJDP Report offers descriptions and realistic assessments of available civil and criminal remedies, explains applicable laws, identifies public and private resources, and identifies strategies to help left-behind parents recover their children or reestablish meaningful contact with them in another country. It covers important developments in policy and practice since the publication of the first edition in February 2002. The guide includes a list of recommended readings; a directory of related resources, including Web sites; a Hague Convention application, with instructions; a checklist for parents involved in non-Hague cases; and an index.
(OJJDP, search "NCJ 215476" at www.ncjrs.gov/App/Publications/AlphaList. aspx, 164 pp.)

Family Reunification After a Lengthy Abduction
This handbook contains information for victims of abduction, their families, and the professionals serving them. The information comes from interviews conducted with adults who were abducted as children. This handbook guides victims, families, and professionals through the often lengthy process of reunification. The handbook also details the experiences of those interviewed.
(NCMEC, www.missingkids.com/en_US/publications/NC23.pdf, 52 pp.)

Kid Gloves for Handling Abducted Children
This publication consists of a multimedia journey through the abduction experience that crafted entirely in the firsthand voices of former abducted children; text chapters that summarize major themes and terms associated with the child's experience of abduction and recovery; and individual guides for left-behind parents, law enforcement, case managers, mental health professionals, guardians ad litem, and judges working with children in cases of family abduction. The guides are also available as individual, stand-alone publications.
(Take Root, www.takeroot.org/publications.html)

Re-Framing Recovery: An Overview of the Kid Gloves Approach to Handling Abducted Children
This paper provides an overview of Take Roots' Kid Gloves Approach. The Kid Gloves Approach is designed to manage a recovery event in a way that minimizes potential new trauma for the child while maximizing the potential to facilitate a healthy transition for and provide assistance to the child from the moment of first contact.
(Take Root, www.takeroot.org/publications.html, 8 pp.)

A Typology of Family Abductions
This paper by Take Root's Executive Director Liss Haviv puts forward a typology for kinds of abduction experiences had by children who are taken by family members, and examines the implications for "recovery" associated with each type. Based on Take Root's program work with hundreds of former abducted children, the paper also take a brief look at points of congruity across different types of cases.
(Take Root, www.takeroot.org/publications.html)

What About Me? Coping With the Abduction of a Brother or Sister
Written by siblings of children who have been abducted, this guide contains information to help and support children of all ages when their brother or sister is kidnapped. The guide provides ideas on what children can expect, the feelings they may experience, the events that may occur from day to day, and the things they can do to help themselves feel better. Written in child-friendly language, it is divided into such sections as: home, family, law enforcement, the media, school and work, and holidays and anniversaries. In addition, the guide contains activity pages for children of all ages, including those who are too young to read.
(OJJDP, search "NCJ 217714" at www.ncjrs.gov/App/Publications/AlphaList.aspx, 69 pp.)

When Your Child Is Missing: A Family Survival Guide (Fourth Edition)

This guide provides parents with the most current information on, and helpful insights into, what families should do when a child is missing. The first edition of this guide was written in 1998 by parents and family members who have experienced the disappearance of a child. It contains their combined advice concerning what to expect when a child is missing, what needs to be done, and where to go for help. It explains the role that various agencies and organizations play in the search for a missing child and discusses some of the important issues that need to be considered. The guide is divided into seven chapters, each of which is structured to allow information to be found quickly and easily. Each chapter explains both the short- and long-term issues and contains a checklist and chapter summary for later reference. A list of recommended readings and a list of public and private resources appear at the back of the guide. This fourth edition of the guide was published in 2010.

(OJJDP, search "NCJ 228735" at www.ncjrs.gov/App/Publications/ AlphaList.aspx, 112 pp.)

You're Not Alone: The Journey From Abduction to Empowerment

This guide presents several stories of child abduction survivors and how they have grown and developed from their traumatic experiences. Written by survivors of child abduction, this guide provides information to help other child abduction survivors cope with their own experiences and begin their journeys toward a better future. Additionally, this guide contains space where readers can write down their own thoughts and feelings in response to each personal story.

(OJJDP, search "NCJ 221965" at www.ncjrs.gov/App/Publications/ AlphaList.aspx, 76 pp.)

U.S. Department of Justice Resources

The **Office of Juvenile Justice and Delinquency Prevention** (OJJDP) provides national leadership, coordination, and resources to prevent and respond to juvenile delinquency and victimization. OJJDP supports states and communities in their efforts to develop and implement effective and coordinated prevention and intervention programs to improve the juvenile justice system so that it protects public safety, holds offenders accountable, and provides treatment and rehabilitative services tailored to the needs of juveniles and their families. Visit the OJJDP Web site at **www.ojp.usdoj.gov/ojjdp.**

The **Office for Victims of Crime** (OVC) was formally established by Congress in 1988 through an amendment to the 1984 Victims of Crime Act (VOCA) to provide leadership and funding on behalf of crime victims. OVC provides federal funds to support victim compensation and assistance programs across the nation. OVC also provides training for diverse professionals who work with victims, develops and disseminates publications, supports projects to enhance victims' rights and services, and educates the public about victim issues. Visit the OVC Web site at **www.ojp.usdoj.gov/ovc.**

The U.S. Department of Justice also supports:

• The **AMBER Alert™ program**, an early warning system to help find abducted children. The AMBER Alert program is a voluntary partnership between law-enforcement agencies, broadcasters, transportation agencies, and the wireless industry to activate an urgent bulletin in the most serious child-abduction cases. The goal of an AMBER Alert is to instantly galvanize the entire community to assist in the search for and the safe recovery of the child. To access the AMBER Alert Web site, visit **www.amberalert.gov.**

• The **National Criminal Justice Reference Service** (NCJRS), a federally funded resource offering information to the public and juvenile justice practitioners. NCJRS is sponsored by a partnership of federal agencies from the U.S. Department of Justice and the Executive Office of the President. It hosts one of the largest criminal and juvenile justice libraries and databases in the world. To access information from NCJRS, or to order or download this publication, visit **www.ncjrs.gov.**

Missing Child Organizations

The **Association of Missing and Exploited Children's Organizations** is a membership organization of nonprofit local agencies in the United States and Canada that provides services to missing children's families. This includes help with poster and flier development and dissemination, advocacy, aid to local law enforcement, and resource referrals. Visit **www.amecoinc.org** or call 1–877–263–2620.

The **National Center for Missing & Exploited Children** (NCMEC) works to prevent child abduction and sexual exploitation; find missing children; and assist victims of child abduction and sexual exploitation, their families, and professionals. To access their resources, call NCMEC at 1–800–THE–LOST (1–800–843–5678) or visit **www.missingkids.com.**

Every state, the District of Columbia, Puerto Rico, and Canada has a **state Missing Children Clearinghouse** that provides support and assistance to families of missing children. A listing of every state clearinghouse is available on the NCMEC Web site at **www.missingkids.com.** On the left side of the page, click on the tab for resources for parents and guardians.

Peer Support

Take Root is a nonprofit organization started by and for former abducted children. Its mission is to respond to child abduction from the unique perspective of the abducted child by raising issue awareness, gathering and sharing knowledge, and facilitating healing. Take Root administers a national peer-support program for adults who were abducted as children, and uses program findings to provide education for multidisciplinary response professionals, victims' families, and the public on the victimology of child abduction and the best approaches to prevention, intervention, and treatment in cases of family abduction. Take Root's vision is to expand our nation's response to missing children *"beyond recovering missing children, to helping missing children recover."* Call 1–800–ROOT–ORG (1–800–766–8674) or visit **www.takeroot.org.**

Team HOPE (Help Offering Parents Empowerment) is a parent mentoring and support program for families of missing children. Made up of parent volunteers, Team HOPE provides mentoring services, counseling, emotional support, resources, and empowerment to parents and families. Volunteers can be reached at 1–866–305–HOPE (1–866–305–4673) or visit **www.teamhope.org.**

CJ's Story

My face was pressed against the window and I was struggling to see inside. I knocked and knocked. I was picking my children up from their summer visit with their Dad, and no one came to the door. Finally, I could see in a window. The apartment was vacant. I went from disbelief to horror to pain and fear. I remember the glass phone booth, calling my attorney and being told to come back home (my ex lived in a city 300 miles away). It was surreal. I could not process what was going on. I couldn't think straight. All I knew is that I wanted my babies.

My story is a little different than others. I located and recovered my children myself. I don't suggest or recommend this. I felt that I needed to do this at the time. But today there are better laws in place, better cooperation among states, more informed and trained professionals, and better resources.

Once my children were back with me, the nightmare didn't end. I spent the next 10 years not knowing, weekend by weekend, if my former husband would kidnap them again. I taught my sons to forgive. I instructed them that they didn't have to always like what we did as parents or even like us, but they must honor us as their parents. I didn't take my sons to counseling. No one even at their school mentioned it. I actually didn't know anyone that had ever been. I just was unaware of what emotionally had happened to my sons. They were home and I just needed to protect them. I had no idea we all needed help. My story, though turbulent and horribly painful, ended in the fact I got my kids back. But my sons, too, have struggled through this and have dealt with it in different ways. Here are the words of one of my sons, who described the ordeal as atrophy.

"If there were one word that best encapsulates the residual effects of this disruption in the normal course of my development, it would be ATROPHY. By definition, atrophy means *the arrested development or loss of a part or organ incidental to the normal development or life of an animal or plant*. And, just like the concentric rings that emanate out from the casting of a stone in water, so too this atrophy radiated out in various areas of my life beyond childhood and well into my adult life, affecting everything from relationships to my own self-image.

"In my case, I was abducted by a parent at the age of three and vividly remember all of my abduction experience. I can still see my father's face and hear his voice telling me that I was unloved and unwanted by my mother and her family. I became plagued by paralyzing fears:

- Fear that I would be taken again and that my security could end again at any moment.
- Fear of the other parent.
- Fear that I was unlikable and unlovable to anyone (save my immediate family).
- Fear that people I loved would die unless I was with them at all times.

"Even after the trauma itself has faded into distant memory, and forgiveness and love have replaced fear and distrust, there are still scars that remain. However, I fight daily to never favor the old wounds."

*I don't know why my mom was able to convince so many friends and family that abducting me was a justified progression in her ongoing battles with my father. Hindsight seems to have clarified for everyone—including my mother—that it was a tragic mistake. I can't help but think how much trauma and heartbreak could have been avoided if those around my mother at the time had recognized her plan for what it was, **an act of child abduction**, and spoken up.*

> —Liss,
>   *former abducted child*

www.ingramcontent.com/pod-product-compliance
Lightning Source LLC
Chambersburg PA
CBHW071623170526
45166CB00003B/1166